DIGESTION

BODYWORKS

Tracy Maurer

The Rourke Corporation, Inc.
Vero Beach, Florida 32964

Tracy M. Maurer specializes in non-fiction and business writing. Her most recently published children's books include the Let's Dance Series, also from Rourke Publishing.

With appreciation to Lois M. Nelson, Paige Henson, Dr. Victoria Brown - Georgia College and State University, and Sharon Vacula.

PHOTO CREDITS:
Timothy L. Vacula: title page, pages 7, 8, 10, 12, 21; © Lois M. Nelson, cover, page 17: © Diane Farleo: pages 13, 18

ILLUSTRATIONS: © Todd Tennyson: pages 4, 15

EDITORIAL SERVICES: Janice L. Smith for Penworthy Learning Systems

CREATIVE SERVICES: East Coast Studios, Merritt Island, Florida

Library of Congress Cataloging-in-Publication Data

Maurer, Tracy, 1965-
    Digestion / by Tracy Maurer.
        p. cm. — (Bodyworks)
    Summary: Describes the parts of the digestive system and how they work to help the body process and use nutrients.
    ISBN 0-86593-584-X
    1. Digestion Juvenile literature. 2. Gastrointestinal system Juvenile literature.
[1. Digestion. 2. Digestive system.] I. Title. II. Series: Maurer, Tracy, 1965-
Bodyworks.
QP145.M38 1999
612.3—dc21   99-23387
                                                                     CIP

Printed in the USA

TABLE OF CONTENTS

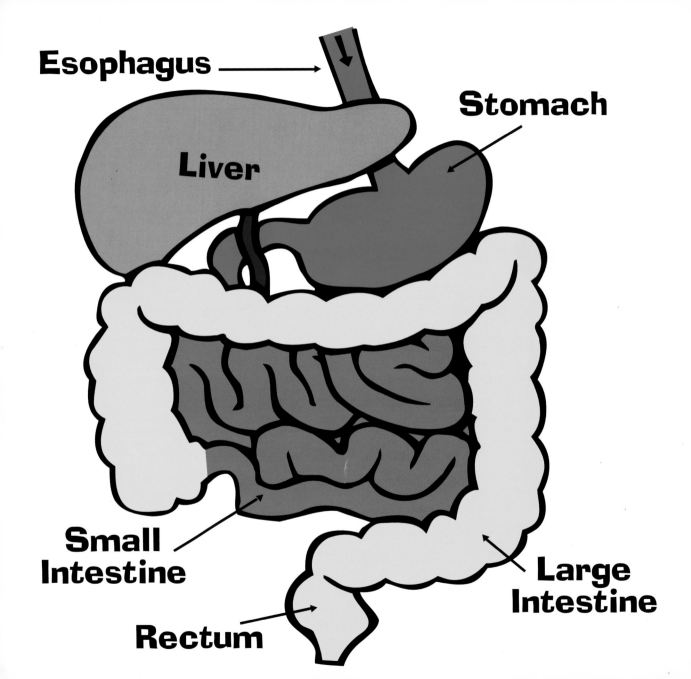

Esophagus

Stomach

Liver

Small Intestine

Large Intestine

Rectum

FOOD FOR FUEL

A car needs fuel to run. You need a full tank, too! Everything you eat and drink fills your stomach. Your body gets the **nutrients** (NOO tree ents) it needs to run smoothly from food.

The **digestive system** (dy JES tiv SIS tem) starts when you chew and swallow food. Many parts inside the body work together to chop, churn, and wring the nutrients from the food. Nutrients become energy for the body and assist with growth. They also help fix broken bones and torn tissue.

The digestive system.

MUSHY FOOD

Teeth tear and grind food. Saliva, also called spit, mixes in. Enzymes in the saliva help break down the food. This makes the pieces easier to swallow.

When you swallow, your tongue pushes food from your mouth to your **esophagus** (es OFF uh gus). Muscles ring this 10-inch (25-centimeter) tunnel. They squish the mushy food down to your stomach.

A small flap covers your windpipe. It keeps food and liquids from going the wrong way. If food or liquid slips into your windpipe, your body quickly coughs it out.

The digestive system begins in the mouth.

ALL MIXED UP

The stomach stretches like a balloon to hold food. The stomach's wrinkled walls unfold as food slides in.

Muscles wrap around the stomach in different directions. They squeeze, twist, and crunch the food. They also help mix in **gastric juices** (GAS trik JOOS ez) that turn the food into a thick soup. Slimy **mucus** (MYOO kus) protects the stomach walls from the gastric juices.

Your stomach works like a kitchen mixer. It churns what you eat into a thick soup.

TWISTING TUBES

The stomach churns a meal for about four hours. Then the soup-like mixture oozes into the twisted **small intestine** (SMAL in TES tin). This 20-foot (6-meter) tube isn't small at all! Here, enzymes break off the food's tiny nutrients. The nutrients pass through the intestine walls and into the blood.

The unused food moves into the **large intestine** (LARJ in TES tin). The large intestine is much shorter than the small intestine. However, it is twice as wide—about 2 inches (5 centimeters) around. The large intestine connects to the rectum. The rectum pushes out lumpy waste when you go to the toilet.

The small intestines stretch out to about the same length as this garden hose!

When you help put away groceries, think of your liver. Part of the liver's job is to store nutrients.

Eating healthy meals keeps your digestive system running smoothly.

THE BUSY LIVER

The football-sized liver performs more than 500 jobs. It aids in digestion by making bile. Bile squirts into the small intestine to help digest fatty foods. The liver also receives nutrients from the small intestine. It uses them to make **proteins** (PRO teenz).

The liver also acts like a sponge as it soaks up and cleans blood. The liver removes poisons, such as alcohol and drugs, from the body.

The liver works so hard that it even makes heat to help warm the body.

In an adult, the liver weighs about 3 or 4 pounds.

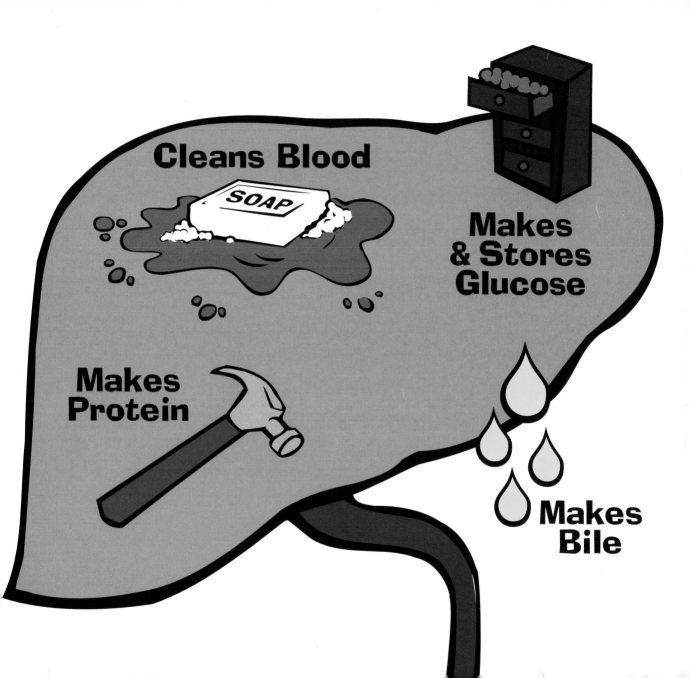

ENERGY TO BURN

The liver makes blood sugar, or glucose. Blood carries this fuel to your cells. The oxygen you breathe lets cells use glucose. This releases energy. Did you know car engines also need oxygen to burn fuel? It's the same idea!

Even when you sleep, your body uses energy from glucose. Activities such as breathing and pumping blood require glucose. Cells also use it for growth and healing. You need a steady supply of glucose. The liver stores extra glucose for use when you need it.

Your body burns extra glucose when you play or when you need to stay warm.

POWERFUL PROTEINS

Proteins form every living cell. Proteins even make the cells that make proteins.

People eat proteins and they make proteins. During a lifetime, the body changes more than 5 tons (4-5 metric tons) of proteins into body parts. These include muscles, skin, and blood.

Humans need to eat about 2 ounces (57 grams) of proteins daily. Even that small amount helps children grow. It gives adults bigger muscles. But, eating too much protein can cause problems. For example, the liver may store the extra nutrients as body fat.

Proteins help muscles grow. Exercise, such as jumping rope, keeps the muscles ready for action.

GOOD FOOD

Scientists study food to understand how the body uses it. They find new clues every day.

Less than a hundred years ago, no one knew what **vitamins** (VY tah minz) were. Now scientists know you need vitamins in your daily diet.

Some vitamins help other nutrients work better. Eating many kinds of food brings these pairs together. Apples make a healthy snack. Eating only apples for breakfast, lunch, and dinner would make you sick, however. You wouldn't get all the nutrients you need.

Eat fruits and vegetables to get important nutrients.

EAT RIGHT FOR LIFE

Meat, fish, eggs, milk, and beans give you proteins. Fruits and vegetables also provide important nutrients, such as vitamins and iron. **Carbohydrates** (KAR bo HI drayts) from cereals, noodles, and breads supply energy.

Eat different kinds of food every day. Sweets and candy bars don't count! Too much sugar may lead to lower test scores in school.

Send a mix of healthy foods through your digestive system every day. It makes your whole body work better.

GLOSSARY

carbohydrates (KAR bo HI drayts) — the parts of cereals, breads, and noodles that give the body energy

digestive system (dy JES tiv SIS tem) — the parts of the body that turn food into fuel

esophagus (es OFF uh gus) — the tube that sends food from the mouth to the stomach

gastric juices (GAS trik JOOS ez) — the thin fluid of enzymes and acids that works in the stomach to digest food

large intestine (LARJ in TES tin) — the short, wide tube that begins at the bottom of the small intestine and ends at the rectum

mucus (MYOO kus) — the body's natural, thick slime that makes food slippery and adds a protective coating for the stomach and other body parts

nutrients (NOO tree ents) — good parts of foods that fuel the body

proteins (PRO teenz) — nutrients found in eggs, milk, beans, fish, and meats; the body also makes its own proteins

small intestine (SMAL in TES tin) — the narrow, long tube that begins at the bottom of the stomach and ends at the large intestine

vitamins (VY tah minz) — the good parts of food that the body needs to stay healthy

INDEX

FURTHER READING:

Find out more about Bodyworks with these helpful books:
• Walker, Richard. *The Children's Atlas of the Human Body.* Brookfield, Connecticut: The Millbrook Press, 1994.
• Miller, Jonathan, and David Pelham. *The Human Body: The Classic Three-Dimensional Book.* New York: Penguin Books, 1983.
• Williams, Dr. Frances. *Inside Guides: Human Body.* New York: DK Publishing, 1997.

On CD-ROM
• *The Family Doctor,* 3rd Edition. Edited by Allan H. Bruckheim, M.D. © Creative Multimedia, 1993-1994.